THE CIRCUS

POEMS

LARRY D. THOMAS

BLUE HORSE PRESS REDONDO BEACH, CALIFORNIA   2016

THE CIRCUS

LARRY D. THOMAS

Blue Horse Press
P.O. Box 7000 - 760
Redondo Beach,
California 90277

Copyright © 2016 by Larry D. Thomas.
All rights reserved.
Printed in the United States of America.

Cover art: Dale Wisely

Editors: Jeffrey and Tobi Alfier
Blue Horse Press logo: Amy Lynn Hayes

ISBN 978 - 0692626405

Other Poetry Collections by the Author

Book-length Collections

2001: *Amazing Grace*, Texas Review Press, Huntsville, Texas

2004: *Where Skulls Speak Wind*, Texas Review Press, Huntsville, Texas

2005: *Stark Beauty*, Timberline Press, Fulton, Missouri

2008: *The Fraternity of Oblivion*, Timberline Press, Fulton, Missouri

2008: *Larry D. Thomas: TCU Texas Poet Laureate Series*, TCU Press, Fort Worth, Texas

2010: *The Skin of Light*, Dalton Publishing, Austin, Texas

2011: *A Murder of Crows*, Virtual Artists Collective, Chicago, Illinois

2013: *Uncle Ernest*, Virtual Artists Collective, Chicago, Illinois

2014: *The Lobsterman's Dream: Poems of the Coast of Maine,* El Grito del Lobo Press, Fulton, Missouri

Poetry Chapbooks

2001: *The Lighthouse Keeper*, Timberline Press, Fulton, Missouri

2002: *The Woodlanders*, Pecan Grove Press, San Antonio, Texas

2007: *With the Light of Apricots*, Lily Press

2007: *Eros, Slow Trains Literary Journal*

2008: *The Circus, Right Hand Pointing*

2009: *Plain Pine*, Right Hand Pointing

2010: *Dark Pearls*, LaNana Creek Press (Stephen F. Austin State University), Nacogdoches, Texas

2010: *Wolves*, El Grito del Lobo Press, Fulton, Missouri

2010: *Five Lavender Minutes of an Afternoon*, Right Hand Pointing

2011: *The Red, Candlelit Darkness*, El Grito del Lobo Press, Fulton, Missouri

2011: *Far (West Texas)*, Right Hand Pointing

2012: *Social Networks*, Right Hand Pointing

2013: *Colors*, Right Hand Pointing

2014: *The Goatherd*, Mouthfeel Press, El Paso, Texas

2014: *Art Museums*, Blue Horse Press, Redondo Beach, California

2014: *The Wadded Up Poem Behind the Dumpster*, Right Hand Pointing

2015: *Los Días de los Muertos*, Right Hand Pointing

Acknowledgments

Special gratitude is extended to Dale Wisely, publisher/editor of *Right Hand Pointing*, in which fifteen of these poems were published in 2008 as an e-chapbook titled *The Circus*.

The author also expresses gratitude to the editors of the following journals in which the poems noted, sometimes in slightly different versions, were first published:

Big River Poetry Review: "To Tricks"

Concho River Review: "The Clown"

descant: Fort Worth's Journal of Poetry and Fiction: "The Carousel Maker," "The Fat Lady," and "The House of Mirrors"

Houston Literary Review: "Unicyclist"

Poetry Depth Quarterly: "Tightrope Walker"

Radiant Turnstile: "Hermaphrodite"

REAL: Regarding Arts & Letters: "A Tented Kingdom of Magic" (published with the title "The Circus")

In memory of Joseph Carey Merrick
(1862-1890)

&

his beautiful cathedral of cards

The attraction of the virtuoso for the public is very like that of the circus for the crowd. There is always the hope that something dangerous will happen.

Claude Debussy

Table of Contents

1. The Big Top

The Big Top	1
The Ringmaster	2
The Clown	3
Tightrope Walker	4
Trapeze Artists	5
Unicyclist	6
To Tricks	7
The Boy in the Stands	8
A Tented Kingdom of Magic	9

2. The Beautiful Animals

The Men in Gray	13
The Animal Trainers	14
Lion Tamer	15
The Dapple-Gray Gelding	16
The Elephant	17

3. The Sideshow

Carny	21
The Carousel Maker	22
The House of Mirrors	23
The Fat Lady	24
Hermaphrodite	25
Siamese Twins	26
The Elephant Man	27
Freaks	28

1. The Big Top

The Big Top

Toward the grinding stars,
to the creaks of winches and pulleys,
they raised it on three huge poles
and secured its edges with iron stakes

sledgehammer-driven
deep into the heart of the earth.
It looms in moonglow, quiet as a tomb
of heavy cloth. In a matter of hours,

at showtime, it will glow in the night
like precious stones roiling in the dark,
cupped hand of a gypsy,
its canvas sides undulant

with the exhaled breath of elephants.

The Ringmaster

He's the commandant of freakdom,
his back so arched it all but rips
brass buttons off his vest. His boot soles
are soiled with the stomped human grime

of fear and doubt. Light dances
in the sheen of his high-topped hat
like the sequins on a gown. Each crack
of his whip drives the stars of his show

closer to the edge of reason. He struts
under the big top, smug in his expertise,
the consummate public relations director
of death. With but the timbre and cadence

of his voice, blessed with the charisma
of a rich evangelist, he works the crowd
to fever pitch and holds it, through the last,
death-defying act, in the palm of his hand.

The Clown

practices his silly acts
in the circus of minutes.
Rainbows snake, kink, and frizzle
from his scalp. It takes him hours

to paint his torturous face,
just to get it sad enough.
Mime is the art that sparkles
in the night show of his life.

His friends are siamese twins,
his bastard child a human
cannonball. For wise counsel,
he eavesdrops the dreams of freaks.

Juggling is his calculus,
slapstick his highest physics.
On the straw of beasts he sleeps.
His mute soul rings with laughter.

Tightrope Walker

A taut, white rope
thrums beneath him
like a noose, unlooped and unknotted.

He looms high above the circus floor,
a daredevil in the spotlight-lit ether
of angels. Each waver of his body

sucks deep gasps from the crowd.
The thrill whips his blood
into epiphany. With a knuckle-

white grip, he grasps his pole
and freezes near the rope's end
as if Balance, his elusive Savior,

may betray him. His slippered feet
clutch the rope like the talons
of a white raptor.

Trapeze Artists

Clad in white, sequined tights
blue spotlights dazzle
into diamonds of muscle,

they scale cotton ladders
to the narrowest of platforms
high above the netless ground.

They flip into the face
of gravity the stiff, insolent
fingers of their bodies.

Powder is their unction,
grip and trust their only gods.
Saved for the last act,

they tantalize the crowd below
gawking, gasping, and ever so
eager for the unexpected fall.

Unicyclist

His cycle's spokes flash
like a giant sparkler.

He pedals its lone wheel
back and forth in jerks

for Balance, his jealous Deity,
in Whom his faith is absolute,

his blind faith a split-second
lapse of which but the coins

of death could compensate,
this acrobat and his one-

wheeled cycle, its handlebar
and other wheel remote

in the sky as the aching,
phantom limbs of an amputee.

To Tricks

the circus owes its magic.
Their mastery allows the clown

to pull ten rabbits from a hat
and to make, intricate as atoms,

the elliptic, intersecting orbits
of the juggler's balls.

In fire issuing from the mouths
of men, they manifest themselves.

It's no wonder they're the biggest draw
of the crowd. Even God plays them.

The Boy in the Stands

loves the circus so rife with color
it's as if he and his naughtiest friends,
armed with jars of finger paint,
were turned loose under the big top,

no holds barred; where gaudiness is religion
and his hated, fastidious sisters,
Misses Prim and Proper, gag from wafts
of sequined elephant dung; where the bosoms

of plumed ladies, stuffed like putty
into their tights, jiggle right before his eyes
for hours on end of slurping sans a straw
or stinging slap; this hallowed place

where his heroes swallow swords
and gorge pure fire; where Danger,
his dark, forbidden friend,
lurks nastily at every turn.

A Tented Kingdom of Magic

The circus is a world of sequins,
dazzle, and endless colored tubes
of light clashing in the sky

like fencers' swords:
a tented kingdom of magic
melding man and animal

into a spectacle
plumed and harnessed to do tricks:
a universe of lions, rearing,

spinning on giant, faceted balls
like plastic ballerinas:
of elephants linked by tail and trunk,

shuddering the earth
like a gray, wheezing freight train
circling rings of freaks

who eke out a living
swallowing the blades of sabers
and eating fire while, high above

the crowd, a helmeted bastard
whizzes through the air, blasted
from the barrel of a cannon.

2. The Beautiful Animals

The Men in Gray

As they labor,
they hum the plodding,
lugubrious bars
of the "Volga Boat Song."

Oddly enough,
they love their drab profession,
tending the entrails
of elephants,

shoveling their tons of dung.
They know that their dreams
issue from the bowels
of their drudgery,

their dreams of white tights
smothered with sequins
brightening their bodies
into gods of cold fire.

The Animal Trainers

In relative obscurity,
they work their black magic.

Their audience
is the eyes of tigers;

Pavlov, the solitary prophet
of their strange, exacting faith.

With cubes of sugar,
they harness the fury of beasts.

Accustomed to the breath
of predators, they execute

their marvelous acts
behind the scenes, satisfied

with their lot as gods
to the men in pretty tights.

Lion Tamer

The lions can smell human fear,
the tamer's only predator. Well-versed
in the lexicon of hunger,

he struts into a cage of flooded light.
The lions, in single file,
flow through a chute like melted wax

and assume their fierce postures
on their stools. The circus air,
thick with the scent of candy and dung,

shatters with the cracks of his whip.
His raised chair looms precariously
between himself and rawest fear.

The lions roar. Their great, flexed paws
swipe blue tubes of light. They leap
through rings of fire, spring back

to their stools, and rear, angling
right between his eyes the double-
barreled shotguns of their muzzles.

The Dapple-Gray Gelding

His great head's fixed downward
as if it grew that way,
his grand plume the horn
of his dream's unicorn.

To stay within the circle,
he was trained to the brink of cruelty.
He performs his act running in circles
with a gymnast on his back.

But for the efficacy of the trick,
his spirit was broken.
Though he runs in circles
with the metronomic rhythm

of a gifted violinist,
the gymnast is the prodigy
for whom the crowd applauds
and he, her dappled Stradivarius.

His broad back's
a table of hot flesh
steady as the teardrop tip
of a dead clock's hand.

Each lap around the ring
emboldens the straight,
endless line
of his desire.

The Elephant

A gray Armageddon of flesh and bone,
sudden as a gunshot under the big top,
it ripped its trunk from the tail of the beast it trailed,
crushed a Volkswagen stuffed with a dozen clowns,

and charged toward the squealing ringmaster.
The children in the stands gasped within their clouds
of cotton candy as their horrified dads
jerked them to the aisles. The ringmaster,

his boot heel entangled in the rung
of a cotton ladder, was swiftly
brought to justice by a tusk. It took
twelve bullets from a high-powered rifle

to end the sequined carnage of a beast
guilty of honoring, in the final,
raging moments of its life, its dormant,
at last awakened vestiges of Africa.

3. The Sideshow

Carny

The Ferris wheel spins in the night sky
like the flywheel of the universe.
He sports a weird tan from countless

hours of exposure to neon suns.
The soles of his shoes are worn thin,
exuding from their cracks the redolence

of popcorn and cotton candy. His face
is the creased leather of a purse
of the poor. Fluent in the language

of thrills and the lure of stuffed animals,
he cocks his mouth, clamps his Camel
in the vise of his lips, and with the sound

of air spewed from a stretched balloon,
manages his irresistible,
"How 'bout another try?"

The Carousel Maker

For permanence,
he renders his horses
in thick, durable plastic,
and, for motion, impales them
with stainless steel poles.

He studs their harnesses
with jewels of frozen fire.
Careful to capture them
at the zenith of life,
he rears them, bares their teeth,

flares their nostrils to the point
of tearing, and, to spark
a little terror in the child,
exaggerates the whites
of their wild, protuberant eyes.

The House of Mirrors

Its vertical surfaces
are concave, convex and wavy,

painted with a smooth film of silver
so pure it's scarcely there.

Its aisles are laid out in a maze.
Its mirrors, the Beatitudes

objectified, are ever giving back
all that they receive.

Having been brought face-to-face
with each monstrous masking

of their guile, the visitors
emerge from it terrified

ad nauseam, baptized
in the horror of their selves.

The Fat Lady

Fine wine and gourmet repasts
fill her ravenous soul like sunlight

sucked through the stained-glass straws
of a sanctuary.

Her mouth enshrines the warm,
sophisticated muscle of her tongue.

The perfect notes of arias
leap from the sheen of her painted lips.

She moves with the fluid grace of waves
lapping the bountiful shores of her presence,

her corpulence a rare white oyster
swaddling the pearl of her dainty skeleton.

Fathoms of lavender silk
straddle her fabulous girth.

Hermaphrodite

He feels the world
with *her* skin and nerves;
love, the allure
of an insoluble puzzle.

It must suffice,
the *it* of a thing
inanimate, finding,
because *it* must,

beauty in the curse
and the monster;
feeling the rush
of the same blood

to the genitals
of a budding man
and woman, fashioned
of the same ounces

of warm flesh
pulsing in the loins
of a freshly pubescent
child, wild with wonder.

Siamese Twins

The darkness is the archive
of their loss where the stars,
grinding to their billions-
of-years-long halts, spin

for a while, spit-shining
their patent leather shoes.
The colorblind philosopher
amuses herself with her Rubik's

Cube of logic, a tone-deaf
organ grinder hard on the heels
of her dark, arbitrary monkey,
while the poet, her brooding twin

with perfect pitch, croons
the dictionary-thick oeuvre
she knows just might, with luck,
get them through the night.

The Elephant Man
(after *The Elephant Man*, 1980, a David Lynch film)

Torchlight, like the yolk of a cracked egg,
trickles down the pockmarked, massive
folds of flesh clinging to a skull
and glints straw stuck in the hair

of a bulbous ear. Breath rattles like air
forced from the folds of ragged bellows.
He spends his days on display
to the gasps and stares of passersby.

Nights, during moments of privacy
allotted him in the squalor of his tent,
he fashions bits of straw into miniature bricks,
and with his mortar of homemade glue,

at the painstaking rate of an inch a year,
raises the walls and spires of his cathedral,
magnificent almost as the mute,
ravishing beauty of his dream.

Freaks

In raw exposure,
they eke out their living,
the extraction of the gasp
their success. Thicker to them

than blood is water,
the stares of strangers
the constants of their lives.
When the show closes,

they hunker down
in the sanctum of their privacy,
and swaddle the terrible
beauty of their souls.

About the Author

Larry D. Thomas, a member of the Texas Institute of Letters and the 2008 Texas Poet Laureate, has published nine book-length collections of poetry and numerous poetry chapbooks, both in print and online. His *As If Light Actually Matters: New & Selected Poems* was published in 2015 by Texas Review Press, Member, Texas A&M University Press Consortium. Thomas's numerous honors and awards include two *Texas Review* Poetry Prizes, two Western Heritage Awards (Western Heritage Museum, Oklahoma), the Violet Crown Book Award (Writers' League of Texas), nomination for the 2007 Poets' Prize (Nicholas Roerich Museum, New York, New York), and eight nominations for the Pushcart Award.

Thomas resided in Houston from 1967 until 2011. He now resides in Alpine, Texas, with his wife, Lisa.

www.ingramcontent.com/pod-product-compliance
Lightning Source LLC
Chambersburg PA
CBHW061309040426
42444CB00010B/2569